Simon Haines

One of Those Days

Ernst Klett Verlag
Stuttgart Düsseldorf Leipzig

Zu dieser Lektüre gibt es eine Kassette
(Klettnummer 570991)

1. Auflage A 1 6 5 4 3 | 2008

Alle Drucke dieser Auflage können im Unterricht nebeneinander benutzt werden. Die letzte Zahl bezeichnet das Jahr dieses Druckes.

Internetadresse: http://www.klett-verlag.de
E-Mail: klett-kundenservice@klett-mail.de

Redaktion: Katherine Inglis-Meyer, M.A.

Zeichnungen: Peter Gray, London.
Druck: typopress Druckerei GmbH, 70771 Leinfelden-Echterdingen.
Printed in Germany.
ISBN 3-12-570990-3

Contents

Chapter 1: A bad start

Charlie woke up suddenly and thought, "Where am I? What day is it? What time is it?" The sun was bright and it was a warm morning. Then Charlie remembered – it was Wednesday: the last day of school.

"Oh, no! I thought I was already in Spain!"

Tomorrow was the first day of the summer holidays and Charlie was going on holiday soon to the Costa Brava – two weeks of sun, sand and señoritas. He didn't want to go to school.

He looked at the clock on the table next to his bed. It was only 6 o'clock. Thank goodness. He still had time to dream of Spain. He put his favourite CD on the CD player and got into bed again. He closed his eyes and listened to the music. He thought about the holidays – the flight to Spain, the beach, the beautiful girls in their bikinis, the disco …

"It's going to be great fun!" Charlie said to himself. "I can't wait."

"Charlie! Where are you? You're going to be late!" It was his mother's voice. "Hurry up!" she shouted.

She said this every morning, so Charlie did not worry.

"Charlie! You have to leave for school in ten minutes!"

"It's OK, Mum," said Charlie. "It's only six o'clock – there's lots of time. I'll get up in a minute or two."

"It isn't six o'clock, Charlie! It's ten to eight! You haven't got time for breakfast now. You have to leave

11 **thank goodness**	Gott sei Dank
15 **beach** [bi:tʃ]	Strand
20 **hurry up!**	beeile dich!

at 8 o'clock. Nicky's had her breakfast and she's ready to go."

"Oh, no!" Charlie shouted and jumped out of bed. "I fell asleep again!"

He put on his school clothes, washed very quickly and ran downstairs.

"Can I have bacon and eggs, Mum?" asked Charlie. "It's going to be a long day at school and I'm hungry."

"You haven't got time for that, Charlie," said his mother. "But here's some toast and jam. You can eat it on the way to the bus stop. I've put a sandwich for the break in your school bag."

"Hurry up, Charlie," said his older sister, Nicky, "We'll miss the bus! And I want to meet Sally before school."

3 **fall asleep** einschlafen

"Oh, yes, of course! Sally! I'm coming!" Charlie ran after Nicky. Sally was in Nicky's year at school and lived next door. She had dark hair like a Spanish señorita and was *very* nice.

Charlie waved goodbye to his mother with his toast in his hand.

"Bye, Mum," he shouted, but he waved too hard and the toast fell on to the street.

"Oh no!" said Charlie "Everything's going wrong this morning! I don't think I want to go to school. I want to go back to bed until the holidays!"

"Oh, Charlie," said his sister. "Don't be so silly! Just hurry up! I can see Sally at the bus stop."

They arrived at the bus stop just as the bus came. So there was no time to talk to Sally.

"Oh, no!" said Charlie for the third time that morning.

"What is it now, Charlie?" said Nicky.

"I've forgotten my school bag!" said Charlie. "I think it was in the kitchen. I must go and get it."

"Silly boy. You'll miss the bus," said Nicky.

"That's too bad," said Charlie. "I need my bag. See you later. Bye, Sally."

Charlie ran all the way home and rang the bell again and again.

"Mum!" he shouted. "I've forgotten my bag!"

But no-one answered. Where was his mother? Then he saw that his mother's car was not there.

3 **next door** nebenan
20 **miss** *hier:* verpassen

Mrs Black, one of the neighbours, saw Charlie and came to her door.

"Have you seen my mum, Mrs Black?" asked Charlie.

"Yes, I have," said Mrs Black. "She left the house a few minutes ago. She was in a terrible hurry. I think she had your school bag in her hand. She got into her car and drove away very fast."

"Oh, no!" said Charlie.

Chapter 2: No bag, no class

When Charlie got off the bus at his school, there were no children in the playground.

"Everyone's in their classrooms. They're already working," Charlie thought.

A car drove out of the school gates very fast and almost knocked him down.

"Are you crazy?" he shouted. Then he saw that it was his mother's car.

"Mum!" he shouted, but she drove so fast that she didn't see him or hear him.

"Oh, well!" said Charlie. "I hope she brought my schoolbag."

6 **knock s.o. down** jemanden umfahren

He went to the school office.

"I'm sorry I'm late," he said to the woman who worked there, Mrs Clark. "I missed the bus because I forgot my bag."

"That's OK," said Mrs Clark. "Your mother was here a few minutes ago. She wanted to give you your bag."

"Did she leave it here for me then?"

"No, she didn't," said Mrs Clark. "I told her you weren't here yet and she wanted to try and find you."

"Oh, no!" said Charlie.

"Don't worry about it now," said Mrs Clark. "I'll telephone your mother and tell her you're here. Go to your classroom."

"OK," said Charlie. "Thanks."

Charlie went to his classroom. He knocked on the door and went into the room.

"Sorry I'm late," he said. Then he looked at the children in the classroom. They were not his friends. They were older children. And this was not his teacher.

"Sorry, you're in the wrong classroom," said the teacher.

"Oh, dear!" said Charlie. "I'm sorry. Nothing's going right for me this morning!"

The children in the class all laughed, and he felt very silly as he quickly left the classroom.

"Where is my class?" he asked himself. "What day is it? Wednesday. Oh, it's swimming today – they're all at the swimming pool – and my swimming trunks are in my bag!"

1 **office** ['ɒfɪs] Büro; *hier:* Rektorat
21 **oh, dear!** o, je!

Just then, Mrs Clark came along the corridor.

"Your mum has just called. She's at home again. Would you like to call her back and ask about your bag?"

"Oh, yes, please, Mrs Clark. Maybe she can bring it now. I need my swimming trunks, too. We've got swimming this morning."

Charlie went back to the office with Mrs Clark and phoned his mother.

"Hi, Mum! Can you come back to the school with my bag, please? I need my swimming things, too."

"I'm terribly sorry, Charlie, but I can't come to the school now. I had a little accident in the car on the way home."

"Oh, no!" said Charlie. "Are you OK?"

"Yes, don't worry about me. I'm fine – but the car is at the garage now, so I can't drive. And I left your bag in the back of the car, too. Sorry!"

"Oh, I see ... Well, see you later. ... What can I do now, Mrs Clark? Mum's had an accident, the car's in the garage and my bag's in the back of the car!"

"Is your mum OK?"

"Yes, but I haven't got my swimming things now," said Charlie sadly.

"Well, the only thing you can do is to go to the swimming pool and sit and watch your friends, Charlie," said Mrs Clark. "You can't sit here. I've got a lot of work to do."

She pushed him out of the office and sat down at her computer.

16 **garage** [ˈgærɑːdʒ] *hier:* (Reparatur)Werkstatt

Chapter 3: Swimming

The swimming pool was behind the school. It wasn't very big, but all Charlie's friends were in the water.

"They're all having a great time," said Charlie to himself. "And I haven't got my trunks with me. I could kick myself."

"Hi, Charlie!" shouted Lenny, his best friend. "Where were you? Why are you late?"

Then another voice called "Hi Charlie!" It was Nathan, another of Charlie's friends. "Are you going to swim with us?"

"No, I can't. I left my bag at home and my swimming trunks are in it," said Charlie. He felt very silly.

"Poor you," said Lenny. "The water's really great."

"Ah, there you are, Charlie," said the teacher, Mr Davis. "What happened to you this morning?"

"I'm sorry, Mr Davis. I missed the bus and then I forgot my bag and then my mum had an accident and then she left my bag in the car at the garage and then I went to the wrong classroom and now I've no swimming trunks and ..."

"Oh, well, Charlie. You can watch the others. That's all you can do. We'll stay here till lunchtime because it's the last day."

Charlie sat down next to the swimming pool. The water looked very cool and very blue. It was a very warm day now.

"I'd really like to have a swim," he thought.

Suddenly Lenny came up behind Charlie and pushed him into the water.

"Have a nice swim, Charlie!" said Lenny.

Charlie went under the water and came up again.

"You idiot!" cried Charlie, "My clothes are all wet!" He climbed out of the swimming pool as fast as he could.

"Don't worry," said Lenny. "They'll soon dry. It's warm today."

"I'm not worried about my clothes," said Charlie. "I'm worried about my watch and my money! I could kill you!"

He listened to his watch.

"Thank goodness, it's still OK. You can thank your lucky stars for that!"

Then he took his wallet out of his pocket. He opened it.

"Oh, no!" he said again. "My money is wet, too!" He looked at a £5 note. It fell into pieces in his hand.

"This is terrible!" said Charlie, "That was the money for my lunch! Now I can't buy any lunch! And I'm really

2 **idiot** ['ɪdɪət] Idiot

hungry. I had no breakfast. And look at my season ticket for the bus! You can't read my name now!"

"Don't worry about the money, Charlie," said Mr Davis. "Lenny can pay for your lunch. He pushed you into the pool, didn't he?"

"But …" said Lenny.

"I don't want to hear anything from you, Lenny," said Mr Davis. "That was not nice. You have to pay for Charlie's lunch, and that's that. You must say you're sorry, too."

"Yes, sir," said Lenny quietly.

Charlie's class all got out of the swimming pool and put on their clothes again. But Charlie couldn't wear his wet things, so he had to find some new clothes. He went to the school office and asked Mrs Clark if she had any old clothes. Sometimes pupils left things at school. She gave him an old pair of trousers and a shirt from her cupboard, but they were too big for him and smelled funny.

Lenny laughed, "You can smell those trousers ten miles away! And you look really funny!"

Charlie gave him a kick. He was quite angry with him.

It was lunchtime now. Charlie and Lenny went to the school dining room and waited in the queue.

"What are you going to have today, boys?" asked Mrs Anderson, one of the women who made the school lunches. "We've got fish and chips, hamburger and chips or pizza and salad."

"I'll have fish and chips," said Lenny.

"Can I have pizza and salad, please?" said Charlie.

10 **sir** Anrede für einen Lehrer oder eine Respektsperson
14 **if** *hier:* ob

"And what would you like to drink?" asked Mrs Anderson.

"Orange juice, please," said Charlie.

"And I'll have water," said Lenny.

Mrs Anderson gave the boys their lunch on trays, and they walked to an empty table. But Charlie's trousers were much too long for him and he fell down. There was pizza and salad everywhere! Lenny started to laugh again.

"Oh no!" said Charlie. "My lunch! And I'm so hungry!"

"You look so funny on the floor with pizza and salad all round you!" said Lenny. Soon everyone in the dining-room was laughing, too.

But Charlie was not laughing. He felt really silly again. This was not his day!

"Don't just stand there! Do something!" he shouted at Lenny. "Stop laughing and help me to pick up my lunch!"

"Sorry, Charlie," said Lenny, "but you are so funny in those old clothes!" He pulled Charlie to his feet and helped him to take back the dirty food to Mrs Anderson, who gave Charlie a new plate. He walked back to the table very carefully and ate his lunch quietly. He didn't want to talk to anyone.

After lunch, Charlie and Lenny went into the playground to play football with their friends. Charlie was the goalkeeper for his team and they won 5–0.

"That's the first nice thing that has happened today," thought Charlie to himself. "So perhaps things will be better this afternoon. I hope so."

5	**tray** [treɪ]	Tablett
12	**was laughing**	lachte
16	**stop laughing!**	hör' auf zu lachen!

Chapter 4: The Maths lesson

At half past one the bell rang. It was time for afternoon school. The first lesson was Maths with Mrs Taylor. Charlie was good at Maths and he liked Mrs Taylor. He really liked to work on the computer, and this afternoon he and Lenny were going to work on their computer project together because it was the last day of school.

"Good afternoon, everyone," said Mrs Taylor. "This afternoon you can finish your projects. If you want any help, put up your hand and I'll come and see you. Have you all got your disks?"

"Yes, Mrs Taylor," said the children all together.

"OK, you can start when you're ready."

"Where's our disk?" Lenny asked Charlie.

"Oh no! " said Charlie. "It's in my bag and …"

"Oh, no!" said Lenny too. "Now we can't do our project! You *are* silly! "

Charlie put up his hand. Mrs Taylor came to their table and asked, "What's the matter, boys? Why aren't you working on your projects?"

"Please, Miss," Charlie explained, "Our disk is in my school bag and my bag is in my mum's car and my mum's car is …"

"You could ring your mum and ask her to bring your bag in," said Mrs Taylor.

"Sorry, she can't," said Charlie. "She had an accident this morning and now her car is in the garage."

"Oh, dear!" said Mrs Taylor. "Is your mum OK?"

"Yes, she's fine," said Charlie, "but my disk is in her car."

18 **what's the matter?** ['mætə] was ist los?

"Oh, don't worry about that," said Mrs Taylor. "You're very lucky. I've copied all the disks. They're safe in my cupboard. I'll go and get yours for you now."

"Great!" said Charlie. "Now we can start working, Lenny."

Mrs Taylor brought the disk, and Charlie put it in the computer. The two boys worked hard on their project until the end of the lesson. They liked working together on the computer.

At the end of the lesson the bell rang and Mrs Taylor said, "Okay, it's time to stop now. Don't forget to save everything. Then take out your project disks carefully and switch off your computers. Put your disks in a safe place, and please don't forget to bring them back to school after the summer holidays."

Then she looked at Charlie and Lenny and said, "Lenny and Charlie, give me that disk, please. Bring your own disk to school after the holidays and I'll copy today's work on to it. OK?"

"OK," said Lenny. "Thanks."

"Oh no!" said Charlie. Everyone in the class turned and looked at him.

"What's the matter now?" asked Lenny.

"It's our disk!" said Charlie. "I can't get it out of the computer!"

"Let me try," said Lenny. He tried but the disk didn't come out. It was stuck.

Charlie put his finger into the computer, but he still couldn't move the disk or get it out.

2 **copy** ['kɒpɪ] kopieren
27 **be/get stuck** [stʌk] klemmen, stecken bleiben

"Don't do that, Charlie," said Mrs Taylor. "The electricity is still on. It's very dangerous. You could hurt yourself or break the computer." She laughed. "You aren't having a very good day, are you, Charlie?" she said.

Charlie looked worried. "What can we do? Will we lose our projects?" he said.

"Don't worry," said Mrs Taylor. "Disks often get stuck in these computers. The school technician will get the disk out for us."

"Thanks very much, Mrs Taylor," said Charlie.

"Have a good holiday, everyone," said Mrs Taylor. "But be careful, Charlie! Don't do anything silly!"

"No, Mrs Taylor," answered Charlie. "I'm going to Spain. That will be nice, I hope. Not like today! Goodbye."

8 **technician** [tek'nɪʃn] Techniker

Chapter 5: The last Art class

Their last lesson was Art.

"I love Art," said Lenny.

"I'm terrible at Art," said Charlie. "I hate it!"

They walked slowly to the Art room. The Art teacher was Mr Collins.

"Hello, boys," said Mr Collins.

"Hi," said Lenny and Charlie.

When all the children were in the class, Mr Collins said, "OK, it's your last lesson before the holidays this afternoon, so you can do oil painting or pottery."

The pupils looked very interested. Oil painting and pottery were two new things for them.

"I'm going to try oil painting," said Lenny to Charlie. "I'd like to be a painter."

"Like Picasso?" said Charlie.

"Yeah," said Lenny. "I'm going to be rich and famous like Picasso!"

"I hate painting," said Charlie. "I'm going to do pottery. I could make my mum a fruit bowl or a vase."

"OK, everyone who wants to do oil painting, stay here in this classroom. Miss Jackson will be your teacher. Everyone who wants to do pottery, come with me."

Charlie and five other pupils went with Mr Collins into the next room. There were a lot of little wheels with seats behind them.

10	**oil painting**	Ölmalerei
10	**pottery** ['pɒtərɪ]	Töpfern
14	**painter**	Maler
19	**vase** [vɑ:z]	Vase

"Right," said Mr Collins. "Sit at one of the wheels. OK? Now, look down at your feet. Can you see a pedal? Push this pedal with your right foot and the wheel will start to turn."

Charlie pushed the pedal with his foot, but nothing happened.

"My wheel isn't turning, sir," said Charlie.

"OK," said Mr Collins. "Sit at a different wheel, Charlie, and try again."

Charlie got up and sat at a wheel next to a girl called Lucy Brown. He pushed the pedal and the wheel started to turn this time.

"That's much better," he said to himself. "And Lucy is nice, too."

"Now, watch me again," said Mr Collins. The teacher pushed his pedal with his foot and the wheel started to turn. Then he took a piece of clay and threw it hard in the middle of the wheel. The clay went round very fast. Mr Collins put his hands in a bowl of water.

"Now, this is the difficult part," said Mr Collins. "Hold the clay with two hands and squeeze it."

Mr Collins squeezed the clay with his hands. The clay changed. It got taller and taller.

"Now try that with your clay," Mr Collins said to the pupils.

Charlie pushed the pedal and the wheel started to turn. He took a piece of clay and threw it at the wheel. But the clay wasn't in the middle of the wheel, so it flew through the air and hit the wall of the classroom.

2 **pedal** ['pedl] Pedal, Trethebel
17 **clay** [kleɪ] Ton, Lehm

"Oh, dear!" thought Charlie. "I'm really silly today."

Charlie took the clay off the wall and tried again. This time the clay went into the middle of the wheel.

"Great," thought Charlie. "Now, what shall I make – a fruit bowl or a vase? A vase, I think."

He put his hands round the clay and squeezed. But he forgot to put his hands in water first, so the clay stuck to his hands.

"Oh no!" said Charlie.

"What are you trying to make, Charlie?" asked Mr Collins.

"A vase for my mum," Charlie said. "But I forgot to put my hands in water first."

"OK," said Mr Collins. "Try again."

Charlie got another piece of clay. He pushed the pedal, then threw the clay in the middle of the wheel. He put his hands into the bowl of water and then held the clay and squeezed. The clay got taller and taller.

"Fantastic," said Charlie. "Look, Mr Collins!"

"Good, Charlie," said Mr Collins. "Now put your hands into the water again."

Charlie took his hands off the clay but he didn't stop the wheel. As he put his hands in the water, the clay flew off the wheel and hit Lucy Brown in the face.

"Oh, I'm so sorry, Lucy!" cried Charlie. "It was an accident!"

Lucy was very angry and ran out of the room to wash her face.

"I'm sorry, Mr Collins," said Charlie. "I don't think I'm very good at this. And it's one of those days! Everything has gone wrong today!"

"Please stop now, Charlie," said Mr Collins. "This is getting dangerous. Perhaps you could buy a vase for your mother."

"Yes, I'll buy one in Spain," said Charlie. He got up and washed his hands. Just then the bell rang. It was the end of the day and the beginning of the school holidays.

"Thank goodness!" thought Charlie as he left the classroom. "It's the holidays at last!"

Chapter 6: Bus problems

Charlie had to wait for the bus. He and his friends stood at the gate and talked about their plans for the summer. Everyone was happy because it was the end of the day and the beginning of the holidays.

"We're going to Scotland for our holiday," said Nathan.

"Send me a postcard of the Loch Ness Monster!" said Lenny. "We're going to Florida to visit my uncle."

"We're going to Spain next week," said Charlie. Then he remembered his mother's accident and he looked worried. "Well, I hope we're going to Spain, but my mum had an accident this morning," he said.

"I'm sure it'll be OK," said Lenny. "Don't worry. Come on, Nathan, we can walk home. It's not far for us. Bye, Charlie. Have fun in Spain!"

"Bye, Lenny, send me a postcard from Disneyland," said Charlie. "Bye, Nathan!"

At the bus stop, Sally, the nice girl from next door, spoke to him. His face got red. He could feel it.

"Hi, Charlie," she said. "Have you had a good day? You missed the bus this morning."

"No … yes … no …" said Charlie, redder than before. "It's been a terrible day. My mum had an accident, too. Did Nicky tell you? Oh … Nicky doesn't know yet! I forgot to tell her."

Sally looked shocked. "Oh, dear! What happened?"

"I don't really know," said Charlie. "The car's in the garage, but I think Mum's all right."

"Thank goodness for that!" said Sally. "Excuse me, Charlie," she asked carefully, "but why are you wearing those big clothes?"

Charlie told her about the swimming pool and Sally said, "That was terrible. You poor thing!"

The bus was late, but Charlie liked talking to Sally and did not look at his watch. He told her about his first pottery lesson and she had to laugh. At half past four a bus came at last. Sally and Charlie got on together and there was a long queue behind them. Charlie showed the bus driver his season ticket, but the bus driver shouted, "That's all wet and I can't read the name! Where did you get this? Did you find it on the street? You can't come on my bus with that! Go and get a new ticket!"

Charlie was now redder than before.

"But it's the last day of school! And my money's in the swimming pool and ..."

"Come on, Charlie," said Sally. "Let's walk home. We don't need this silly bus."

The bus driver was angry but he did not say any more. They got off and started to walk home together. Charlie was quite happy because now he could talk to Sally for half an hour. Great! And she didn't laugh because he had dirty old clothes on. Not like his friend Lenny. She was *really* nice.

So they walked and talked, and talked and walked. But after about five minutes a car stopped and the driver opened the window. It was Mrs Taylor, Charlie's Maths teacher.

"Where are you two going?" she asked. "Would you like a lift?"

"That's very nice of you, Mrs Taylor," said Sally. "We're walking home because Charlie's season ticket was wet and the bus driver couldn't read it. We live in the same street."

"Come on then, get in, the two of you," said Mrs Taylor. "I know Charlie's had a bad day today. I'll take you home."

12 **about** — *hier:* ungefähr
12 **driver** — Fahrer/in
16 **would you like a lift?** — möchtet ihr mitfahren?

Chapter 7: The bathroom window

Mrs Taylor stopped her car at Charlie's house.

"Here we are," she said. "I hope you have a good holiday, Charlie. Where do you live, Sally?"

"I can get out here too, Mrs Taylor," said Sally. "I live next door to Charlie. Thanks for the lift."

"Yes, thanks very much, Mrs Taylor," said Charlie. "Goodbye."

He stood at the garden gate with Sally and said quickly, "Would you like to come in to see Nicky? We could have some lemonade or tea or crisps or something ..."

"Yes, why not?," said Sally. "It's the last day of school and I won't see her much in the holidays."

Charlie looked for his key in his pockets, but it wasn't there. "Oh, no!" he said.

"Have you lost your key?" Sally asked Charlie.

"No, not really," said Charlie, "but it's in my school bag and my school bag is in Mum's car, and Mum's car is at the garage. Remember? But Nicky must be in. Or my mother. I'll ring the bell."

He rang the bell for two or three minutes and then he knocked on the door. No one answered.

"Perhaps your mum's at the garage," said Sally.

"And Dad's still at work, of course," said Charlie. "But where's Nicky?"

"Perhaps Mrs Black next door has got a spare key. I'll go and ask her. Then you could wait for Nicky. She won't be long," said Charlie. He went to the neighbour's house and knocked on the door, but Mrs Black was out, too.

25 **spare** [speə] **key** Ersatzschlüssel, zweiter Schlüssel

"Oh, dear! What can we do now?" said Charlie. He began to feel silly again. He really had bad luck today.

"Perhaps there's an open window," said Sally. "Let's have a look."

"The bathroom window is sometimes open, but that's upstairs," said Charlie.

"Well, you could take a ladder and climb in," said Sally.

They went to the back of the house and looked up.

"Yes!" said Charlie, "It *is* open. Fantastic! Let's get Dad's ladder."

They found the ladder at the end of the garden. It was quite heavy, but they carried it to the house together and put it up to the bathroom window.

"OK," said Charlie. He didn't like ladders and was a bit scared, but he couldn't tell Sally that. "You can hold the ladder and I'll climb up."

2 **bad luck** Pech

"Right," said Sally. "This is a real adventure!"

Charlie climbed slowly up the ladder and then climbed in carefully through the bathroom window. Suddenly someone shouted "Help!" It was a woman's voice and it came from the bathroom. There were more funny noises and doors banged.

"Oh, dear!" thought Sally. "What's happened? Who's there? Poor Charlie, everything's gone wrong today!"

A few minutes later, Charlie came to the front door with a *very* red face.

"I'm sorry, Sally. Can you come another time to see Nicky, please. That was my mum. She fell asleep in the bath and didn't hear the bell."

"Of course, Charlie. I'm sorry. I hope your mum isn't angry with us. I'll phone Nicky tonight and perhaps we can go for a picnic together tomorrow. OK?"

"Great," answered Charlie. "See you tomorrow then."

He watched her go out of the garden gate and thought, "Thank goodness, not *everything* went wrong today."

5 **funny** *hier:* komisch, seltsam
6 **bang** knallen

Activities

1. Word game

a) Charlie is Nicky's _ _ O _ _ _ _ _ .
b) At school Charlie went into the _ _ _ N _ classroom.
c) Charlie's mother had an _ _ _ _ _ E _ _ in her car.
d) Charlie is going on _ O _ _ _ _ _ to Spain.
e) Lenny and Nathan are Charlie's F _ _ _ _ _ _ .
f) Charlie is terrible at _ _ T . He hates it.
g) Charlie and Sally carried Dad's ladder together because it was very H _ _ _ _ .
h) Charlie climbed into the house through the bathroom _ _ _ _ O _ .
i) Nicky is Charlie's S _ _ _ _ _ .
j) Mrs Black is Charlie's _ E _ _ _ _   _ _ _ .
k) Charlie had pizza and _ _ _ _ D for his lunch.
l) Mrs Taylor is Charlie's _ A _ _ _ teacher.
m) Charlie wanted to make a vase out of _ _ _ Y .
n) Lenny _ _ S _ _ _ Charlie into the pool.

2. School timetable

Here is a school timetable for one day. Copy it and then fill it in with your favourite subjects.
Here is a list of subjects:

Maths / Art / English / German / Biology / History / Science / P.E. / Geography / Music ...

9–10	10–11	11–11.30	11.30–12.30	12.30–1.30	1.30–2.30	2.30–3.30
		Break		Lunch		

3. Finish the sentences

a) In Spain Charlie wants to meet …
b) When Charlie got to school …
c) When he got out of the swimming pool …
d) Lenny had to pay …
e) In the game of football …
f) Charlie's disk was …
g) In the art lesson Charlie wanted …
h) Charlie's clay flew off the wheel …
i) Mrs Taylor gave Charlie and Sally …
j) Charlie's Mum fell asleep …

… Charlie's clothes were wet.

… a lift home in her car.

… Charlie's team won 5–0.

… in the bath.

… there was nobody in the playground.

… to make a vase for his mother.

… beautiful girls in bikinis.

… for Charlie's lunch.

… stuck in the computer.

… and hit Lucy Brown in the face.

4. Right or wrong?

a) Charlie wanted bacon and eggs for breakfast.
b) Sally had fair hair.
c) Charlie's mum had to go to hospital after her accident in the car.
d) The swimming pool was two miles away from the school.
e) Charlie had pizza and salad for lunch.
f) Charlie hated Maths and he hated his Maths teacher.
g) Charlie hit Mr Collins in the face.
h) Sally spoke to Charlie at the bus stop on the way home.
i) The bus driver shouted at Charlie because his season ticket was wet.
j) Charlie fell off the ladder.

5. One of those days!

Do you sometimes have days like Charlie? What sort of things happen to you then? Write a few sentences for your *diary* and describe a bad day.

Here are a few phrases to help you:

The alarm didn't go off ...
My bicycle was ...
The bus / train / tram was late ...
I forgot my Maths book ...
I had to go back home for ...
The English teacher was angry because ...
I lost my money when ...
A big boy hit me in the ...
...
My boyfriend/girlfriend ...
My father ...

6. Titles and endings

a) Can you think of another *title* for the story? Work in groups and then choose the best one in the class.
b) Can you think of a different *ending* to Charlie's day? Work in pairs and then discuss your ideas with the rest of the class.

7. Art

Draw a *picture* of your favourite scene in the story. Choose the best pictures and hang them up in the classroom.

8. A play project

Work in groups. Choose one chapter or scene that you like and make a little play out of it. Here are a few tips:

★ First, write out the *dialogue* for the **characters* (Charlie, Lenny etc.). Use the words of the story. How many people are there in your play?
★ Decide who will *act* in the play.
★ Read out the new dialogue in *parts*.
★ Learn the dialogue at home.
★ One person can be the **producer*.
★ One person can do *sound effects* (e.g. the noise of Charlie's tray when it falls).
★ One person can read the text if someone forgets their part.
★ You can write a *programme* for the class.
★ Act out the play in class.

Have fun!

character ['kærəktə] Person in einem Theaterstück
producer [prə'dju:sə] Regisseur

Lösungen

1.

a) BR**O**THER b) WRO**N**G c) ACCID**E**NT
d) H**O**LIDAY e) **F**RIENDS f) AR**T** g) **H**EAVY
h) WIND**O**W i) SI**S**TER j) N**E**IGHBOUR
k) SALA**D** l) M**A**THS m) CLA**Y** n) PU**S**HED

3.

a) In Spain Charlie wants to meet beautiful girls in bikinis.
b) When Charlie got to school there was nobody in the playground.
c) When he got out of the swimming pool Charlie's clothes were wet.
d) Lenny had to pay for Charlie's lunch.
e) In the game of football Charlie's team won 5–0.
f) Charlie's disk was stuck in the computer.
g) In the art lesson Charlie wanted to make a vase for his mother.
h) Charlie's clay flew off the wheel and hit Lucy Brown in the face.
i) Mrs Taylor gave Charlie and Sally a lift home in her car.
j) Charlie's Mum fell asleep in the bath.

4.

a) right; b) wrong; c) wrong; d) wrong; e) right;
f) wrong; g) wrong; h) right; i) right; j) wrong.